OSIEN SIBANDA

P*The*ARABLES *of* JESUS
30 DAY DEVOTIONAL

GW00801840

SIBANDA
PUBLISHING

Dedication

I warmly dedicate this book to the GHIC
church family in Bristol and Yeovil. You are an
immense inspiration and blessing to me. I pray
that we may continue to love the Lord our God
and to serve Him for the rest of our lives.

Acknowledgements

S pecial thanks go to my precious wife and long-time friend, Fatima Sibanda. You are such a blessing to me and I thank God for you. Thank you for all your hard work and for editing this work vigorously. To my two lovely daughters, Ayanda and Realeboga, you enrich my life and I am proud to be your dad.

To Sarah Masengo and Loulita Gill, thank you for all your hard work in designing and preparing this devotional for printing. God bless you. To Kemi Abanishe and everyone who took time to edit and proof read the manuscript, thank you. God bless you. To all who will take time to read and all who will recommend this book to others, thank you in advance. As you read this book I pray that the Lord will minister to you in a special way. May God bless you all.

CONTENTS

INTRODUCTION

A parable is defined as a short story that teaches a moral or a spiritual lesson. It is a word that originates from the root word *"paraballo"* or from the Greek word *parabolē* and Latin word *parabola*. The word paraballo can be split into two: *"para"* meaning to compare or to come along side and *"ballo"* which means "to throw". These also mean a metaphor, a proverb or an adage.

Among the things that are easily imprinted in our memory are songs and stories. This is because we engage more with them than we do with a list of instructions. Jesus used parables during his ministry in order to teach certain concepts. This was so that His audience would gain better understanding of what he taught by relating to the stories used. (**Mark 4:33**). Various principles were taught through this medium including lessons about good conduct versus bad conduct, sinful behavior versus godly behavior, the Kingdom of heaven versus the kingdom of darkness. After teaching in parables Jesus would often ask His audience to take heed to what they heard.

This devotional has been written to help us to glean valuable lessons from these parables. To inspire, enlighten, educate, remind, as well as teach us from the wisdom of the one wiser than Solomon, Jesus Christ the Messiah. It is my prayer that we learn from this simple but well written book and gain more knowledge and understanding as King Solomon advises us in **Proverbs 4:5-7** *"In everything we acquire we should aim to gain more understanding."*

1

A FRIEND IN NEED

"*Then Jesus said to them, 'Suppose you have a friend, and you go to him at midnight and say, "Friend, lend me three loaves of bread; a friend of mine on a journey has come to me, and I have no food to offer him." And suppose the one inside answers, "Don't bother me. The door is already locked, and my children and I are in bed. I can't get up and give you anything." I tell you, even though he will not get up and give you the bread because of friendship, yet because of your shameless audacity he will surely get up and give you as much as you need.'*" **(Luke 11:5–8)**.

Jesus used this parable to emphasise the importance of asking for help when we are in need. In verse 9 He says, "*So I say to you: ask and it will be given to you.*" In this illustration, a friend visited a friend because another friend had visited him. The friendship was the reason to meet this need. Even though it was night-time, he was confident that the bond of friendship would enable him to receive help.

This man kept knocking and banging on the door that had been locked for the night. Jesus then said that the reason the friend got up to help was not because of the friendship, but because of the persistent knocking on the door. Sometimes we disqualify ourselves from blessings because we give up when we come across locked doors. Jesus says to knock regardless, because those who locked the door are able to hear you, and they have the ability to open it.

Our love for our friends will compel us to keep knocking until help arrives. We must not give up too soon. It is obvious that at midnight people are usually in deep sleep. Knocking lightly for a short while will not get you anywhere. Jesus is advising to knock until something happens: *"yet because of your shameless audacity, he will surely get up and give you as much as you need."* Sometimes we don't receive answers because we are not persistent.

When you are in need, it is your responsibility to look for help. Zacchaeus was in need, and he did something to attract the attention of Jesus: *"He wanted to see who Jesus was, but because he was short he could not see over the crowd. So he ran ahead and climbed up into a sycamore-fig tree to see him"* (**Luke 19:3-4**). Jesus saw his effort and invited Himself to his house, and Zacchaeus' need was met. The hindrance in this case was his height. In the first story the hindrance was a locked door.

We must learn to see through locked doors and press through our physical limitations if we want our needs met. Blind Bartimaeus had a serious need, and he also wanted a friend who could help him, but certain doors were locked. Here is how his need was met: *"When he heard that it was Jesus of Nazareth, he began to shout, 'Jesus, Son of David, have mercy on me!'"* Bartimaeus was quiet all along, but when he realised potential help was nearby, he started knocking on the door. He did not stop until Jesus heard him. Although the crowds were telling him to be quiet, he knew his need and finally was able to say, *"Rabbi, I want to see"* (**Mark 10:46–51**). He pushed past his limitation and received his sight.

Ask, seek and knock; do all you can until you receive from God. Don't give up easily. We have learnt that it sometimes takes banging on doors, climbing of trees and even shouting over the crowds to receive what we need. We need to be persistent and not quit.

REFLECTION TIME

Do you give up easily? Are you impatient? Pray for resilience in your daily life. Do not be easily discouraged. Keep on pursuing your God-given dreams.

2

THE FOUR TYPES OF SOIL PART 1

"*A farmer went out to sow his seed. As he was scattering the seed, some fell along the path, and the birds came and ate it up. Some fell on rocky places, where it did not have much soil. It sprang up quickly, because the soil was shallow. But when the sun came up, the plants were scorched, and they withered because they had no root. Other seed fell among thorns, which grew up and choked the plants. Still other seed fell on good soil, where it produced a crop – a hundred, sixty or thirty times what was sown.*" (**Matthew 13:3–8**).

Jesus interpreted the seed as the Word of God, and the different types of soil as the different heart attitudes with which people respond to the Word of God. These four types of people exist even today, and we must ensure that the seed of the Word we hear grows into plants that will yield righteousness.

When we hear the Word and do not understand it, the enemy comes to snatch it away because we do not perceive its value. We do not see it as a treasure so we do not water it or take it seriously because we are occupied with other things. This is like the seed that fell on the path. The path is a busy place, where many things are going on. It is very easy to be distracted by what is happening on the path. The heart on the path did not bother to water the seed, and the enemy snatched it away. Paul teaches us an important principle: "*I planted the seed. Apollos watered it, but God has been making it grow*" (**1 Corinthians 3:6**). There are many times when we do not water the Word because we have not understood it.

The Berean Church is a good example of seed waterers: *"Now the Berean Jews were of more noble character than those in Thessalonica, for they received the message with great eagerness and examined the Scriptures every day to see if what Paul said was true"* (**Acts 17:11**). When our attitude is like this, the enemy has no chance of snatching the Word.

In the book of Hebrews we learn about two churches that received the same Word. One achieved results, but in the other, the seed just fell on the path: *"For we also have had the good news proclaimed to us, just as they did; but the message they heard was of no value to them, because they did not share the faith of those who obeyed"* (**Hebrews 4:2**). This confirms that they did not understand the significance and the importance of that Word, so they let it slip outside of their hearts, and the devil came and stole it.

If we understand the value of the Word, we will hide it in our hearts. *"I have hidden your word in my heart,"* David says in **Psalm 119:11**. Jesus also presents the Word as a hidden treasure that must be found and preserved by those who understand its value: *"The kingdom of heaven is like a treasure hidden in a field. When a man found it [or understood it], he hid it again and then in his joy went and sold all he had and bought that field"* (**Matthew 13:44**). The idea of hiding the treasure is to stop the enemy from snatching it away!

A good example of the path or the "wayside" heart (NKJV) is the rich young ruler in **Matthew 19:16–22**. He had come to Jesus looking for eternal life: *"Teacher, what good thing must I do to get eternal life?"* Jesus gave him the Word that eternal life was to be found in following Him, not in the abundance of the money the man had. So the first step was to get rid of the mind-set he had followed for years, hoping it would give him eternal life. Hence Jesus' response: *"Go, sell your possessions and give to the poor, and you will have treasure in heaven. Then come, follow me."* This was the Word, but it fell on the path.

We must note that Jesus never told the young man to give **all** the proceeds to the poor. He merely said to go and sell what he had, and also to give to the poor. Because the man did not understand the Word, he lost out on the eternal life he was looking for.

REFLECTION TIME

Pray that you may understand the Word that is preached. Believe it and value it, otherwise you will lose it. Take the Word seriously and meditate on it. That way, the enemy cannot steal it from you.

3

THE FOUR TYPES OF SOIL
PART 2

"*A farmer went out to sow his seed. As he was scattering the seed, some fell along the path, and the birds came and ate it up. Some fell on rocky places, where it did not have much soil. It sprang up quickly, because the soil was shallow. But when the sun came up, the plants were scorched, and they withered because they had no root.*" (**Matthew 13:3–6**).

Jesus gives the interpretation of the second type of soil in **Matthew 13:20–21**: "*The seed falling on rocky ground refers to someone who hears the word and at once receives it with joy. But since they have no root, they last only a short time. When trouble or persecution comes because of the word, they quickly fall away.*"

Rocky ground refers to shallow soil resting on a bed of rock. Jesus said such a person has no root in Him. This person has very little soil because there is too much rock underneath. The joy with which they receive the Word cannot be sustained because there is nowhere for the Word to take root. The nature of the Word is that it must find root in our hearts for it to yield the required results. **Colossians 2:6–7** teaches, "*So then, just as you received Christ Jesus as Lord, continue to live your lives in him, rooted and built up in him.*" You cannot be rooted if there is rock under the soil in your heart.

To be firmly rooted, we have to break up the rock so that there can be more soil to facilitate the growth of the roots. We must take action to deal with rocky hearts because they have the potential to thwart the growth of the Word. Jeremiah addressed Israel when they had rocky hearts. He told them to "*Break up your unploughed ground and do not sow among thorns*" (**Jeremiah 4:3**).

Shallow ground is hard and stony; it is not ideal for sowing seed. The good thing is that it can be broken! Break it up. Break up the hard ground, remove the stones and bring in fresh soil. The children of Israel had been hardened by sin and idolatry. These are the stones that mess up our hearts. We must learn to deal with them so that the Word can take root in our hearts.

Rocky ground has no depth, which means that seed cannot go deep to secure roots because there is very little soil. The plant shoots up quickly because that is the only way to go, but the sun is ready to scorch the plant that is not rooted. When tribulations and persecutions come, we stumble and fall because we do not have enough roots to hold us up.

As believers, we must learn to cultivate and break up the soil of our hearts so that our roots can go deep. Failure to deal with the rocks in our hearts exposes us to the risk of being scorched when heat comes. We are also told that the thief comes to steal. He steals the Word.

Growing up on a farm helped me to understand the significance of this parable. After sowing, birds would come and try to dig out the seeds and eat them. Seeds that fall on shallow soil risk being eaten, losing their potential. Seeds that have shallow roots fail to build up the strength necessary to hold the tree firmly in the ground. The water and nutrients required for growth come from the ground, and if all the ground we have is stony, we are doomed to be scorched! Break up your unploughed ground and make your heart receptive to the Word.

REFLECTION TIME

Is your heart hard? Ask the Lord to help you to have a tender and teachable spirit. Pray against doubt and unbelief. Rid yourself of any unforgiveness, bitterness, pride and self-righteousness because they are some of the rocks that hinder the development of roots. Continually till your heart in prayer.

4

THE FOUR TYPES OF SOIL PART 3

"Other seed fell among thorns, which grew up and choked the plants." (**Matthew 13:7**).

The interpretation of the thorny soil is given in verse 22: *"The seed falling among the thorns refers to someone who hears the word, but the worries of this life and the deceitfulness of wealth choke the word, making it unfruitful."*

From this we can tell that the thorny environment is the pressure of the world. Jesus cites the cares of this world as the first problem, and the deceitfulness of wealth as another one that can choke the Word. According to Jesus, this type of person hears the Word and then thorns spring up and choke the Word. In other words, priorities change because of preoccupation with things of the world. These rise up and eventually become more important than the Word.

The deceitfulness of wealth means that we are focused on riches to the extent that we begin to be driven by them, forgetting the Word. These are thorns. Jesus, addressing this problem, warned, *"Be on your guard against all kinds of greed; life does not consist in an abundance of possessions"* (**Luke 12:15**). This is emphatic: Jesus wants us to take heed and beware of the deceitfulness of riches, as they can choke the Word!

When the Word is choked, we become barren and unfruitful in spiritual matters, even though our initial instruction at the time of creation was to be fruitful and multiply (**Genesis 1:28**). We must take heed of thorns in our hearts because there are many cares in this world today. Labels! What trainers are you wearing?

What brands of clothing do you like to wear? What phone do you have? Have you seen this movie? Have you driven the X5? Have you been to this or that famous place? What qualifications do you have? How big is your house? Who is in your social networks? Did you take a selfie with this or that celebrity? The list goes on and on. These things will choke the Word, and Jesus said we must be careful.

Greed is another type of thorn that the church must not accept. It normally comes in the guise of material blessings. Some churches have been consumed by the desire to acquire material wealth. Take heed! the Word is being choked, and soon you will be unfruitful. The problem with greed is that it never feels greedy. A new phone that is not needed is seen as just an upgrade. Anything in excess, from food to the latest fashions, can easily become a care. If these start to drive us, and we give them too much value, they will choke the Word and move us away from the heart of God.

Paul instructed Timothy to warn the church about thorns: *"Command those who are rich in this present world not to be arrogant nor to put their hope in wealth, which is so uncertain, but to put their hope in God, who richly provides us with everything for our enjoyment. Command them to do good, to be rich in good deeds"* (**1 Timothy 6:17–18**). Good works come about as a result of good application of the Word. If the Word is choked, the good works will not come forth.

In **1 Timothy 6:9**, Paul shows another side of this thorny tree: *"But those who desire to be rich fall into a temptation and a snare, and into many foolish and harmful lusts which drown men in destruction and perdition"* (**NKJV**). Drowning is equivalent to choking, in that they both take away life. They block the free flow of air and you become unfruitful. We cannot nurture the Word of God in a thorny heart because there will be too much competition. The last part of **1 Timothy 6:10** says that those who have been deceived by riches have *"pierced themselves with many griefs"*.

Reflection Time

What thorns have been trying to choke the Word in your heart? What is your value system? Take some time to prayerfully examine your life. If you identify any thorns, pluck them out. Ask God to help you to guard your heart against the cares of this world. Ask for the grace to focus on that which has eternal value.

5

THE FOUR TYPES OF SOIL
PART 4

"Still other seed fell on good soil, where it produced a crop – a hundred, sixty or thirty times what was sown." (**Matthew 13:8**).

Jesus, in His interpretation said, *"But the seed falling on good soil refers to someone who hears the word and understands it"* (**Matthew 13:23**). This indicates that understanding is good ground. We must understand the Word in order to be fruitful. Understanding is defined as perceiving the meaning of something, or to have an idea of it. It also means to be thoroughly familiar with or to apprehend clearly.

Proverbs 4:7 encourages us to gain wisdom and understanding in all things: *"Though it cost all you have, get understanding."* What does it take to understand the Word of God? We must ask the Holy Spirit to teach us the Word. When we read, we should pray for revelation and understanding. We must also have faith that God will do what He says.

Bible tools such as Vines Expository Dictionary are important tools for us to check meanings of words and understand the proper context. In addition, good Bible commentaries are excellent investments to broaden our understanding. It is also recommended to compare different (respected) versions of the Bible to help us understand what we are reading. And we can ask for help from those who lead us if we are failing to understand a portion of Scripture that we are reading. Attending church regularly and being part of small group fellowship and mentoring groups give us opportunities to share and discuss the Word with others to gain clarity and deepen our understanding.

It is our responsibility to get understanding. Once we have understood, we can apply what we have understood in our daily lives. That way, our relationship with God begins to yield righteousness in us.

David said, *"Your word is a lamp to my feet, a light on my path"* (**Psalm 119:105**). This understanding helped David to navigate his way in life, with the Word being the lamp and light to guide him. He also meditated on God's Word: *"Blessed is the one ... whose delight is in the law of the Lord, and who meditates on his law day and night"* (**Psalm 1:1-2**). Because he knew the benefits of reading the Word and having it as the source of his guidance, David meditated on it day and night. When we understand the Word and apply it, we become fruitful, as Jesus mentions in the parable. David understood this when he commented about the man who understands the Word: *"That person is like a tree planted by streams of water, which yields its fruit in season and whose leaf does not wither – whatever they do prospers"* (**Psalm 1:3**). James teaches us to be doers of the Word (**James 1:22**), but we cannot "do" the Word if we do not understand it. This is why we must get understanding.

All along, the intention of the farmer in this parable was to plant his seed on good ground. Jesus is looking for hearts that will understand the Word, as this is the only ground that gives a yield. All the other types of soil failed to produce because they failed to understand the value and significance of the Word. In the end, they were barren and unfruitful. Jesus concludes the parable by saying, *"Whoever has ears, let them hear"* (**Matthew 13:9**). What we must hear is that we ought to be good ground for the Word. We must seek to understand the things of God.

In **Luke 24:45** we read that Jesus opened the minds of his followers so they could understand the Scriptures. Understanding Scripture is a spiritual thing. Not everybody understands the Scriptures. We must prayerfully read and study the Word in order to understand it. The apostle Peter encouraged husbands to live with their wives *"with understanding"* (**1 Peter 3:7, NKJV**). Understanding will always be fertile ground for any relationship, be it with your family, your friends, your employer or your God. **1 Chronicles 12:32** tells us about the importance of understanding and how this helped King David: *"From Issachar, men who understood the times and knew what Israel should do – 200 chiefs, with all their relatives under their command."* That same understanding can help you know what to do with the Word of God and how to handle life.

REFLECTION TIME

Ask God to open your mind so that you may understand the Scriptures. Invest in Bible tools that will help you to understand the Word. Attend meetings and services where you will be taught the Word. You cannot understand the Word if you do not take time to read it and listen to it being preached or taught. Pray before you read the Word and ask the Holy Spirit to teach you and to help you to understand.

6

NEW WINE IN OLD SKINS

"Neither do people pour new wine into old wineskins. If they do, the skins will burst; the wine will run out, and the wineskins will be ruined. No, they pour new wine into new wineskins, and both are preserved." (**Matthew 9:17**; see also **Mark 2:22** and **Luke 5:37–38**).

One might ask, "Was Jesus a wine maker?" "Where did He learn about wine and wineskins?" This metaphor was drawn from the day-to-day culture of Jesus' times. A wineskin containing new wine would stretch as the wine continued to ferment. After that, the skin would harden. This was now an old wineskin because it had gone through the process of making wine and hardening through the fermentation process. If new wine was put into an old and hardened wineskin, the fermentation process risked bursting the old wineskin.

The idea was to make new wineskins every time new wine was made. This could be costly, but it was the right way to do it in order to preserve both the wine and the wineskins.

Generally, people don't want to give up familiar and comfortable habits and customs, particularly when something has been part of them for a long time. This is especially true with regard to religion and moral issues. The temptation is to try and plug part of our old ways into the new experience or religion. This is what happened to the Galatian church. The Jews wanted to force the Gentiles to be circumcised in order to be Christians. This was a form of pouring new wine into old wine skins. Paul had to rebuke them vehemently because the church risked losing the Gentile brethren. (**Galatians 3:1–3**).

The point Jesus was making was that the message and gospel He was bringing could not be made to fit the old order and old forms of religion that were familiar to the Jews – issues such as circumcision and sacrifice of animals and only worshipping from the Temple in Jerusalem. Forcing those traditions on people would be like forcing them into an old wineskin and would result in the church losing these brothers. *"Neither circumcision nor uncircumcision means anything; what counts is the new creation"* (**Galatians 6:15**). The new creation comes with its own values and standards, focusing on the heart and not the flesh.

Jesus introduced who he was to the people of His time. He taught them the principles of the kingdom of God and Kingdom conduct. He demonstrated that he was the Messiah, the way, the truth and the life. He taught them that He was the Son of God and the giver of eternal life. *"Very truly I tell you, unless you eat the flesh of the Son of Man and drink his blood, you have no life in you. Whoever eats my flesh and drinks my blood has eternal life, and I will raise them up at the last day"* (**John 6:53–54**).

This is the new wine that Jesus was bringing, and it required new wineskins to contain it without bursting. Old minds that used to eat sheep and cow flesh could not contain this.

The Jews needed to understand the new role Jesus had come to play, but they kept comparing Him with the old: *"Are you greater than our father Abraham?"* (**John 8:53**). *"Are you greater than our father Jacob, who gave us the well and drank from it himself, as did also his sons and his livestock?"* (**John 4:12**). These were the old wineskins failing to recognise the new wine in Jesus. They wanted to hold on to the old. But Jesus said, *"I am the way and the truth and the life,"* and, *"Before Abraham was born, I am!"* (**John 14:6; 8:58**).

REFLECTION TIME

What old wineskins are you trying to fill in your life? Ask God to open your eyes to the new things He brings to your life by His Spirit. Are there things you are holding on to from your past? Are you mixing the ways of a born-again Christian with worldly ways? Ask the Lord for the grace to let go of past worldly or religious methods. Embrace your walk with God fully, and walk in His ways.

7

THE UNFRUITFUL FIG TREE

"**H**e also spoke this parable: *"A man had a fig-tree growing in his vineyard, and he went to look for fruit on it but did not find any. So he said to the man who took care of the vineyard, 'For three years now I've been coming to look for fruit on this fig-tree and haven't found any. Cut it down! Why should it use up the soil?' 'Sir,' the man replied, 'leave it alone for one more year, and I'll dig round it and fertilise it. If it bears fruit next year, fine! If not, then cut it down'""* (**Luke 13:6–9**).

The fig tree was planted in a vineyard because the owner wanted some figs. After three barren years the master wanted to cut the tree down. His main problem was that the tree was using up the soil but not producing figs. It was not serving its purpose.

We must be fruitful in the kingdom or we will be cut off. Jesus warned us about the importance of this in **John 15:1–2**: *"I am the true vine, and my Father is the gardener. He cuts off every branch in me that bears no fruit, while every branch that does bear fruit he prunes so that it will be even more fruitful."* God wants fruit from the Word we read in our private times and from the Word we hear Sunday after Sunday. He is always looking for fruit.

The gardener promised to dig around the fig tree and fertilise it in order to assist it to be fruitful. There are many ways that the Lord digs around us to fertilise us because He requires fruit from us. **Matthew 3:8** tells us, *"Produce fruit in keeping with repentance."* God always wants fruit out of us as a result of applying His Word in our daily lives.

The question the master asked was, *"Why should it use up the soil"* when it is not producing fruit? Have you ever imagined that the Lord will ask you why you wasted His talents, His gifts and even His grace? The Bible speaks to us about God's expectations: *"From everyone who has been given much, much will be demanded; and from the one who has been entrusted with much, much more will be asked"* (**Luke 12:48**). The fig tree had been given much in that it had been planted in the vineyard where it received special care and protection. In spite of all this, it could not produce fruit. There was a lot of investment in this tree and the master had every right to be unhappy if it was just taking up space in the garden for nothing.

That is a question that can easily be directed towards us? Are we productive? Are we fruitful? Do we do as much as we can to preach the Word? Are we bearing fruit with the talents and abilities that we have? Much has been given to us, and much is expected.

The fig tree was given one more year. We don't know when the Lord last measured our progress, but we must learn to dig up and fertilise ourselves for fruitfulness.

REFLECTION TIME

Have you been fruitful in your life as a believer? What can you dig up to make you more fruitful? What forms of fertiliser do you require to enrich your soil? The master expects fruit from the life, gifts and talents He has given us. Ask God for the grace to be a tree that produces good fruit all the time.

8

THE COST OF DISCIPLESHIP

"Suppose one of you wants to build a tower. Won't you first sit down and estimate the cost to see if you have enough money to complete it? For if you lay the foundation and are not able to finish it, everyone who sees it will ridicule you, saying, 'This person began to build and wasn't able to finish.' Or suppose a king is about to go to war against another king. Won't he first sit down and consider whether he is able with ten thousand men to oppose the one coming against him with twenty thousand?" (**Luke 14:28–31**).

Jesus introduced this parable when He was talking about the cost of following Him, and the cost of discipleship. It was difficult to be a follower of Jesus during His days on earth. Those who followed Him had to consider the cost.

The essence of discipleship is giving Christ first place. There are pressures from Satan in the form of temptations; there are pressures of family life, or from workmates, and from people who might not understand the lifestyle of a believer. This parable highlights the commitment required in order to be a true disciple. How many people have you known who started on this journey and have gone back? Jesus wanted us to take heed lest we fall and backslide after having preached to others. We must be determined to finish well as disciples. Jesus wants us to consider the fact that some of our friends and relatives will not accept our decisions about following Him.

We need to make personal choices about following Jesus, and count the cost. We should not let anyone decide for us, because at the end of our lives we will stand as individuals before the judgement seat (**Romans14:11–12**). Each of us will give an account of himself to God. Hence the importance of weighing the cost of our decisions and actions. Our final destination in following Jesus is when we meet Him and spend eternity with Him. That is a successful disciple. Paul tells us of some who started and failed, like Alexander the coppersmith and Demas (**2 Timothy 4:10–14**). We don't want to be like them.

Our daily lives consist of choices that we make. Before embarking on something we must sit down and count the cost. Any major or life-changing decision calls for careful consideration. We should not plunge into things blindly because we have not stopped to count the cost. The consequences of not weighing situations may be dire, and even at times irreversible. As disciples and followers of Christ, we must continue to hold on to our faith no matter what challenges we face. We cannot afford to draw back. Let us learn from the example that Jesus gave us if we are to "build a tower" successfully. That way we will be able to put structures in place to succeed. This could be through prayer, study, good company, or getting rid of certain associations. Sitting down to consider will help us bolster our mission as disciples. We should get rid of the leaven that could affect us.

Reflection Time

Have you ever suffered the consequences of a decision you made without counting the cost? Do you know of anyone who started well in the faith but has now stopped following Jesus? Have you started some projects and stopped halfway because you did not weigh the cost? How are you doing as a disciple, and what is it costing you? Pray and ask God to help you to be a true disciple no matter where you are or where you go in life.

9

THE TWO SONS

"What do you think? There was a man who had two sons. He went to the first and said, 'Son, go and work today in the vineyard.' 'I will not,' he answered, but later he changed his mind and went. Then the father went to the other son and said the same thing. He answered, 'I will, sir,' but he did not go. Which of the two did what his father wanted?" (**Matthew 21:28–31**).

The first son was abrupt in his answer. Although he was talking to his father he answered negatively. We do the same at times, especially when we are angry or disappointed. Sometimes this leads to lost opportunities and we miss our blessing. We must learn to pay attention when those in authority speak to us because sometimes God will be testing our obedience.

Abraham was tested! *"Do not lay a hand on the boy ... do not do anything to him. Now I know that you fear God, because you have not withheld from me your son, your only son"* (**Genesis 22:12**). God does test us sometimes, to prove us. The first son in the parable almost failed the test, but he quickly realised his mistake and rectified it: *"But later he changed his mind and went."* This was the turning point in his life because, from here, he did his father's will. Jesus always emphasised doing the Father's will. In **John 4:34** Jesus said that His food was to do the will of His Father. He confirms this in **John 5:30** and in **John 6:38** where He says, *"For I have come down from heaven not to do my will but the will of him who sent me."*

This parable teaches us about a young man who almost forgot the position of his father, but quickly realised and repented. We may not always be given an opportunity to repent, so it is better to obey immediately. Five of the ten virgins in **Matthew 25:1–13** did not get such an opportunity.

The actions of the second son resemble what many of us normally do. We are quick to promise to do right but fail to execute our promises. This is worse than the actions of the first son because people take us at our word and are then disappointed when we do not keep it. Imagine what would have happened if the father had gone away and left every responsibility with such a son? He failed the test his father had given him.

James encountered such people, hence the teaching that he gave in his epistle. *"But be doers of the word,"* he said in James 1:22 (NKJV). The word to the young man was *"Go and work today in the vineyard."* He heard the word and promised to do it, but he never did. Jesus commented about such sons and disciples: *"These people honour me with their lips, but their hearts are far from me"* (**Matthew 15:8**).

We do this often, and Jesus warned that this is why we will miss out on the promises of God and the treasure of the kingdom. God wants us to take His instructions seriously. We must be a people who believe in our God and understand that there is a purpose and destiny in everything He wants us to do. If we fail to realise this, we will miss out on things God has planned for us. Jesus warned that tax collectors and prostitutes would enter the kingdom before the teachers of the law, who had been hearing the Word over and over without obeying. Many promise to obey but fail in application. Harlots and tax collectors repented when they realised their mistakes, and they were received. *"Truly I tell you, the tax collectors and the prostitutes are entering the kingdom of God ahead of you. For John came to you to show you the way of righteousness, and you did not believe him, but the tax collectors and the prostitutes did. And even after you saw this, you did not repent and believe him"* (**Matthew 21:31–32**). It's important to realise our mistakes and rectify them. This is what Jesus is saying.

REFLECTION TIME

What do you do when you realise you have made a mistake? Your attitude and actions are crucial to your walk. God wants us to repent and believe when we hear the Word or see the truth. Ask God to help you to be a person who acknowledges your wrong. Pray that God may deliver you from a spirit like that of the second son, who just obeyed with his lips. Pray that you will be diligent to listen to instructions and respond promptly in faith and in obedience. Pray that the Lord will help you to be sincere in all things.

10

THE PRODIGAL SON

"There was a man who had two sons. The younger one said to his father, 'Father, give me my share of the estate.' So he divided his property between them. Not long after that, the younger son got together all he had, set off for a distant country and there squandered his wealth in wild living." (**Luke 15:11–13**).

This boy is likely to have been an unmarried teenager. Custom dictated that a younger son would receive half of what the older son would receive, or a third of his father's estate. This son knew his rights and demanded what was rightfully his when he thought he was ready to manage it. Was this the right time for him to claim that right? Another question to ask is, do we have to claim our inheritance or it will be passed on to us at a specific time? The most ideal time would have been when the father was deceased or about to die or when he saw it fit.

The early Jews warned fathers about breaking and distributing an estate too early. In this case the father granted the request, illustrating how God permits us to use our own will. God sometimes allows us to have what we want because He wants us to learn to choose wisely; according to the laws He has given.

Verse 13 says he spent everything in wild living, wasting his possessions in careless living. He spent senselessly until his money was finished. He was not as mature as he thought. The Bible warns against that as well: *"For by the grace given me I say to every one of you: do not think of yourself more highly than you ought, but rather think of yourself with sober judgment"* (**Romans 12:3**). God will never shout from the heavens to stop us from making wrong choices. We must think soberly; we must count the cost of our choices. God has given us His Word to guide us in all things.

Proverbs 28:7 says, *"A discerning son heeds instruction, but a companion of gluttons disgraces his father."* The younger son had gluttonous companions who helped him waste his father's hard work on useless things. The shame he brought upon his father was in the choices he made. When his money ran out, he went to feed swine, and in the process ate from the same trough. This was shameful to a Jew! Jews considered swine to be unclean animals. This son had gone from a loving home to a disgraced state where even his father's workers would not tread. This all started when he thought he knew better.

The young man's way led to near death! He salvaged his life by swallowing his pride, repenting and going back home. What a humiliating experience for a man who once thought so highly of himself. We must be careful about our ego and carnality – they can easily lead us astray. In his new life back home, he had no claim on anything; he expected nothing but being a servant. A hot meal was suddenly more valuable than his pride! He had been humbled and was now fully dependent on his father's grace. This is the right place to be in our relationship with our Father. We should always depend on Him.

The young son was clearly immature, yet he thought he was capable of surviving alone. He was very ambitious. We must be careful about our thoughts and ambitions. Philippians 4:8 teaches us what to think about in order not to go astray. We are safer in the presence of the Father, not away from Him. We must also be careful about the friends we choose because they can lead us astray, only to turn against us when we are in trouble. *"You will fill me with joy in your presence, with eternal pleasures at your right hand"* (**Psalm 16:11**). I am sure the young son learnt this in the end.

REFLECTION TIME

Ask the Lord to help you to abide in His presence always – that is your safety zone. Pray for patience in everything you do. Be careful of the decisions you make and watch out for wrong influences. Pray for wisdom and discernment in all things.

11

THE PRODIGAL SON 2

"*Meanwhile, the elder son was in the field. When he came near the house, he heard music and dancing. So he called one of the servants and asked him what was going on. Your brother has come, your father has killed the fattened calf because he has him back safe and sound.' The elder brother became angry and refused to go in.*" (**Luke 15:25–28**).

The older son remained with the father all the time that the younger son was wasting his life. This made him think he was more deserving and closer to his father. He was the special one and thought he should be informed about everything that was in the father's heart. He now thought the father ought to consult him on how to conduct his business. The father had chosen to slaughter a fattened calf to celebrate his second son's safe return home. We are not told that he slaughtered a calf that belonged to the older son.

The attitude of the older son equates well with that of the Pharisees' attitude of self-righteousness, pushing other people away as sinners. In verse 29 he begins to compare his acts of righteousness with the sins of his brother. He wants the father to judge from his perspective: But the father always operates from a father's heart. The older son was actually transgressing the father's commandment of love, even though he thought he had never transgressed the father's commandments. The father had given a command for a calf to be slaughtered. The father had given a command for the family to have a feast, yet the older brother "*became angry and refused to go in*" (verse 28).

The Message version says, *"The older brother stalked off in an angry sulk and refused to join in. His father came out and tried to talk to him, but he wouldn't listen."* Here is a man who is blatantly disregarding his father's decisions, yet he claims to have never disobeyed! This is the prodigal son in the father's house! At this point in the lives of the two sons, the younger son is more in the will of the father, even though he has just been home for a few hours. The one who thinks he has it all wrapped up is actually lost! What a tragedy when we do not understand the father's heart.

The unhappiness of the older brother illustrates the response of the Pharisees and the scribes at the prospect of sinners becoming acceptable to God. They did not like it. They were offended by the fact that people who had been sinning for years just repented and Jesus received them. They wanted to see them punished! God's plan is to give everyone a chance to repent before facing judgment at the end of life. We must learn and know the heart of God if we are to please Him. The older son was working against his father. He shamed his father by challenging his decisions before the servants.

Both sons brought shame to the household in one way or another. We must be careful about this. I may not fail in the same way my brothers fail, but I do fail. There is no failure that is greater than another. All have sinned and come short of the glory of God. For some it's lying; for some, lust; others, murder; some, backbiting; some, hypocrisy; and for yet others it is just a failure to do what they know is right. All is failure before God and requires us to look into our hearts, to get on our knees and to say, "Father, I have sinned against you."

The contrast between the older son's attitude and that of the younger son on their return home is crucial. Both were returning to meet the father. One was on his knees repenting and the other was challenging his father in arrogance. After serving for so many years, he failed at the last hurdle. The older son proclaimed his righteousness, and argued that justice had not been done.

REFLECTION TIME

Have you ever thought you have served God more than others? Is there a time when you thought your faith was better than that of others? Have you ever compared yourself to others and thought you were better? This is the time to watch out, for your test is around the corner. Ask the Lord to help you not to judge others. Pray for the grace to celebrate the blessings of others.

12

THE PRODIGAL SON 3

The ability to make wise decisions is crucial, especially when it involves family feuds. We must always endeavor to make decisions based on what is right, not who is right. Blaming others for their mistakes will not help us make good decisions. Looking for what is right is the most spiritual thing. This sense of rightness comes from the nature of God. God is Righteous! What is right comes from God.

The father in this parable concludes with wise words to his elder son: *"But we had to celebrate and be glad, because this brother of yours was dead and is alive again; he was lost and is found"* (**Luke 15:32**). We must learn to do what is right all the time. **James 4:17** teaches, *"If anyone, then, knows the good they ought to do and doesn't do it, it is sin for them."* The father shows his elder son the right way to live.

In verse 27, the servant raised the importance of relationships to the older son, and the point he made was, "This is your brother; you guys are brothers!" The father could have said, "He is my son just as you are; I cannot let him stay outside." Instead, the father reiterated the servant's message of relationship between the two to make it more personal for the older brother to understand. Personalizing our relationships makes it easier for us to be sympathetic and compassionate. When we learn to personalize our relationships, we will value and celebrate people in spite of the challenges we may face. Our relationships should be more important to us than our personal conflicts.

The father viewed the younger son's departure from home as a form of death: *"dead ... alive ... lost ... found"*. The total transformation of the young son is summarized in these two contrasts. As far as the father was concerned, such transformation was reason enough to celebrate. This is also why Jesus chose to associate with the lost. They are better off at home, so when they make steps towards salvation, they should be encouraged and celebrated.

The father accepted his son's confession but refused his son's request to make him a servant: *"Father, I have sinned against heaven and against you. I am no longer worthy to be called your son; make me like one of your hired servants"* (verses 18–19). The father refused this request, yet he had accepted the initial request of his portion of the inheritance. This is a father's heart. Wealth and possessions cannot compare with sonship. The father was not prepared to put his son on the same level as his servants just because of money.

This is why God sent His Son for us. We are too precious in His eyes to remain in sin and under the oppression of the enemy. *"For God so loved the world that he gave his one and only Son, that whoever believes in him shall not perish but have eternal life"* (**John 3:16**).

We may not think we are like these two sons, but we often are. God has already given us standards by which to conduct our lives, but we often choose our own ways. When the Bible tells us, *"Do not be drunk on wine,"* and we continue to drink, we are actually saying, "Give me the portion of the inheritance that belongs to me." We are saying, "I don't want to live by these conditions; I want to go to a far country." When we continue in sinful habits and willfully disobey God we are actually in a pigpen. Many of us are not humble enough to go home because we do not realize we are eating with pigs.

The father saw his son as having died, and therefore receiving him back was a cause for celebration. This shows us the difference between the father and the older brother. The father saw his son as lost. The brother, on the other hand, saw someone who was arrogant and proud and who should suffer the consequences of his decisions. There should be a father's heart in every family, and that is the heart that unifies the family members. If we lose the father's heart, we will lose one another.

REFLECTION TIME

What type of heart do you have, particularly when there is conflict around you? Is there any area in your life where you might be eating with pigs? How do you relate to your natural and spiritual siblings? How about your natural and spiritual parents? Ask the Holy Spirit to help you to embrace both your natural and your spiritual family unconditionally.

13

THE AMBITIOUS GUEST

"When he noticed how the guests picked the places of honour at the table, he told them this parable: 'When someone invites you to a wedding feast, do not take the place of honour, for a person more distinguished than you may have been invited. If so, the host who invited both of you will come and say to you, "Give this person your seat." Then, humiliated, you will have to take the least important place. But when you are invited, take the lowest place, so that when your host comes, he will say to you, "Friend, move up to a better place." Then you will be honoured in the presence of all the other guests."* (**Luke 14:7–10**).

In ancient times, the best seats at a meal or a feast were reserved for those closest to the host. Jesus knew this, and He taught this parable after observing people violating this understanding: *"he noticed how the guests picked the places of honour at the table"*. He realised that people were eager to elevate themselves. They were keen to raise their social status and wanted to impress others, which Jesus did not like. He took it upon Himself to correct them.

"When someone invites you to a wedding feast, do not take the place of honour." Jesus was warning them so that they would not be hurt when they were demoted. This parable is about wisdom and humility. The key to this message is in verse 11: *"For all those who exalt themselves will be humbled, and those who humble themselves will be exalted."*

As people of God, we must watch out for self-exaltation. We must realise that there are more honourable people than us, so we must be humble. Jesus understands the pain of humiliation and embarrassment in public, hence this teaching. In this passage Jesus tells His listeners what to do and how to behave when invited.

Among the listeners here were Pharisees, and most of Jesus' parables were at least partly directed at them. Jesus once rebuked them for self-exaltation: *"Woe to you Pharisees, because you love the most important seats in the synagogues and respectful greetings in the market-places. Woe to you, because you are like unmarked graves, which people walk over without knowing it"* (**Luke 11:43–44**).

The Pharisees walked with Jesus for years but failed to humble themselves before Him. Humility is a grace that is expected of every believer, but it takes a lot of "dying to self" to be humble. In everything we do, Jesus wants our motives to be pure and right. Sometimes we fight over things because of our egos. It is important for us to humble ourselves and allow God to lift us up. Jesus warns that we risk the possibility of being forcefully humbled if we fail to learn this lesson.

REFLECTION TIME

Are you self-exalting and proud? It's time to examine yourself and begin to walk in humility. Do you see yourself as more deserving than others? How ready are you to take that low seat? Pray and ask God to help you to live by Jesus' instructions. Do not blow your own trumpet; rather let others blow it for you.

14

YEAST

"*Jesus told them still another parable: 'The kingdom of heaven is like yeast that a woman took and mixed into about thirty kilograms of flour until it worked all through the dough.'*" (**Matthew 13:33 – NIVUK**)

The Message version says, "*God's kingdom is like yeast that a woman works into the dough for dozens of loaves of barley bread – and waits while the dough rises.*"

Yeast is an essential ingredient in many bakery products. It has been used for the past 5,000 years or so and is responsible for leavening dough and for imparting a delicious flavour of yeast fermentation. It is believed that having good yeast and using the yeast properly makes the difference between success and no success in a bakery operation (dakotayeast.com).

In the parable, the woman works yeast into the dough and waits for it to influence the dough, ensuring an end product that is tasty and beautiful. Jesus likens the kingdom of God to yeast in the world: it must rise and influence it. Although leaven sometimes symbolises evil, here the kingdom of heaven is compared to the dynamic nature and character of yeast. When yeast is kneaded into the dough, it expands and influences the entire batch of dough. The Bible tells us not to be conformed to this world but to be transformed (**Romans 12:2**). Yeast transforms what it comes into contact with. The Bible also says we are the light of the world: when we show up, darkness must flee.

Isaiah 61:3 says, "*They will be called oaks of righteousness, the planting of the Lord for the display of his splendour.*" The kingdom of God must spread and transform whole communities. Darkness must not surpass light where there are people of God. The church must learn to knead its godly leaven into its communities and influence them towards godliness.

Jesus said, *"Whoever believes in me, as Scripture has said, rivers of living water will flow from within them"* (**John 7:38**). The Holy Spirit must flow from within us to transform us and those who come into contact with us. (**John 15:7–8**). Disciples of Jesus are like yeast that should spread and give a flavour of godliness to the world. The kingdom is like yeast. You are like yeast, and you must impact lives by your godly lifestyle.

REFLECTION TIME

What type of yeast are you? How are you influencing your family, friends, community and nation? Pray and ask God to help you to be a positive and godly influence to those you interact with on a daily basis, starting with your family.

15

THE GREAT BANQUET

" Jesus replied: 'A certain man was preparing a great banquet and invited many guests. At the time of the banquet he sent his servant to tell those who had been invited, 'Come, for everything is now ready.' But they all alike began to make excuses. The first said, 'I have just bought a field, and I must go and see it. Please excuse me.' Another said, 'I have just bought five yoke of oxen, and I'm on my way to try them out. Please excuse me.' Still another said, 'I have just got married, so I can't come.'" (Luke 14:16–20).

In the ancient times, invitations to such events were sent out a long time in advance. We are told that this was a great banquet, but certain people opted to abstain because they regarded their affairs as more important. We do this a lot of times when it comes to the kingdom of God and church involvement. Excuse after excuse! What we are saying really is that our lives and programmes are much more important and greater than the kingdom of God. Prayer meetings and church services are neglected, yet things of interest like football, television and social networks are always given time.

One person wanted to see his newly bought land. Another wanted to try his new oxen, and the last one claimed that he had just got married. The Old Testament exempted a man from military duty because of marriage (**Deuteronomy 20:7**), but not social events. In the account in **Matthew 22:5** we are told that, *"they paid no attention and went off"*. The Message version says that, *"They only shrugged their shoulders and went off."* How many times do we shrug our shoulders and move away from the things of God? How many times do we give excuses? Jesus is aware of our attitudes, hence this warning and teaching.

The challenge here is that this was a great banquet that would not come again. We must learn to put aside our agendas when the Lord calls us to His feast. Land can be seen another time because it has already been purchased; the same applies to the oxen. They are already yours and can be checked on another day. Marrying a wife means she is now yours till death separates you; you can easily take her to the banquet with you if you really want to go. Excuses will not help on Judgement Day.

After all the excuses from the invited guests, the master then called people from the streets to eat at the banquet, but there was still room for more. Verse 24 says, *"I tell you, not one of those who were invited will get a taste of my banquet."* Even though there was still room, those who gave excuses would not be permitted if they tried to attend after they had finished their business.

It is worth noting that it is not just sin or the rejection of the gospel that we must avoid. This parable shows that procrastination and the habit of giving excuses is equally dangerous. These are some of the main reasons why Jesus is not preached and followed today. May the teaching in this parable wake us up to the fact that there is something more important than our earthly achievements. Theft, lying, infidelity and immorality no doubt slay people in their thousands. But decent, plausible, smooth-spoken excuses slay tens of thousands more. No excuse can justify a man in refusing God's invitation and not believing in Christ. Remember that Jesus has always been inviting us: *"Come to me, all you who are weary and burdened, and I will give you rest"* (**Matthew 11:28**). Yet we still give excuses! **John 7:37** says, *"Let anyone who is thirsty come to me and drink."* Yet we still give excuses!

This parable warns us that the time will come when God will withdraw His invitation and offer it to others. Then it will be too late to get into the banquet. Let us not be too busy for God; this is a great banquet and we do not want to miss it.

Reflection Time

What have been your excuses concerning your relationship with God? Is there anything that you have considered to be greater than the Kingdom of God? It's time to reflect. Do you do things that you deem to be more important than what God is calling you to do for Him? Ask God for the grace to be diligent in serving Him. Repent from a life of excuses.

16

THE MUSTARD SEED

"What shall we say the kingdom of God is like, or what parable shall we use to describe it? It is like a mustard seed, which is the smallest of all seeds on earth. Yet when planted, it grows and becomes the largest of all garden plants, with such big branches that the birds can perch in its shade." (**Mark 4:30–32**).

A mustard seed is much smaller than the seed of corn or a grain of wheat, yet its growth is highly spectacular, reaching a height of ten to twelve feet. It grows much bigger than other plants with much larger seeds. The point of this parable is not how things begin. It does not matter how small your beginning is. The important thing is the potential that is within you – that is what you must learn to focus on. The mustard seed has great potential, but it must be planted and allowed to grow. We need to put certain things in the ground and allow the potential within to grow.

In the parable of the mustard seed, the key is the comparatively large result from such a humble and seemingly insignificant beginning. Jesus had little support from the religious community of His time when He came to earth. He was like a mustard seed. As time went on, He became a massive tree that still stands today. We all find shelter under His name. His branches are all over us. **Proverbs 18:10** says, *"The name of the Lord is a fortified tower; the righteous run to it and are safe."* But this began as a mustard seed. The Bible teaches us not to despise the day of small beginnings (**Zechariah 4:10**), because it may just be a mustard seed.

The Message version says that eagles nest in this mustard tree. Eagles do not build their nests just anywhere. They look for tall trees that will not make it easy for predators to reach their young. The fact that birds are nesting in this tree shows the significance of its size. The kingdom of God is like that. It may start small but, given time, its full potential is realised because it comes from a great God. David says in **Psalm 48**, *"Great is the Lord, and most worthy of praise."* Everything about the kingdom of God has the potential to be great, including you and your children. You have great potential, even though it may not appear so at times. All you need is to be planted in the right place, and you will begin to grow.

It is important for you to understand your potential. This will help you to be patient. This will enable you to trust God. Do not complain or doubt your potential because your seed might still be small. In you there is a massive tree whose branches will shoot out. When the birds nest in you, they will not even know how small your seed was. They will be glad you are big enough for them to build a nest. As a child of God, learn to look beyond your seed. For in every seed there is a blessing of fruitfulness and greatness, and you are a part of that. The seed of the righteous will prosper and be blessed.

Reflection Time

Do you have areas of your life that you feel are insignificant? Take them to the Lord and ask Him to help you to wait on Him. You will grow to be a blessing. Do not underestimate yourself. You were made in God`s image, and the greater one resides in you.

17

THE FISHING NET

"Once again, the kingdom of heaven is like a net that was let down into the lake and caught all kinds of fish. When it was full, the fishermen pulled it up on the shore. Then they sat down and collected the good fish in baskets, but threw the bad away. This is how it will be at the end of the age. The angels will come and separate the wicked from the righteous and throw them into the blazing furnace, where there will be weeping and gnashing of teeth." (**Matthew 13:47**).

Other versions of the Bible call this a dragnet. The idea was that it would be dropped to the bottom of the sea and then dragged along, catching anything in its way. That is the nature of the kingdom, according to Jesus. There are all sorts of creatures in this net, but the fishermen's focus is on the good fish. Sometimes we wonder about the attitudes of certain people in the church, but Jesus teaches us that we should not worry because the sorting out will be done on the shore.

It does not mean that everything in the net is good! The warning we must heed is that there will be a screening session where the good will be separated from the bad. Another Scripture which supports this is **Matthew 7:21.**

As believers it is always our responsibility to make sure we qualify to be selected among the good fish. Jesus suggests that the only way we can call Him Lord and be accepted into the kingdom is by doing His will. Calling Him Lord and not doing His will is a way to disqualification. Doing the will of the Father will make us the good fish in the net of the kingdom.

The lesson to learn from this parable is not to worry about the different types of people in this net. They will be taken care of by those authorised to do so in the end. Another point to remember is that it will always be uncomfortable to be squeezed in a net with different people, but through this net is the way to be selected. We must focus on doing the will of the Father. That is the only way we will escape the lake of fire.

REFLECTION TIME

What is your attitude to those in the kingdom with you? Ask the Lord to help you to focus on yourself and your heart as the net is dragged along the bottom of the sea. Focus on the selection criteria and ask God to help you make it in the end. Be willing to do His will and to walk in His ways.

18

VALUABLE TREASURE

"The kingdom of heaven is like treasure hidden in a field. When a man found it, he hid it again, and then in his joy went and sold all he had and bought that field. Again, the kingdom of heaven is like a merchant looking for fine pearls. When he found one of great value, he went away and sold everything he had and bought it." (**Matthew 13:44–45**).

These two parables are a verse long each, and their focus is on the worth of the kingdom. In the first one, the man just stumbles upon this treasure hidden in a field. He hides the treasure again because he recognises its value. Whoever hid it the first instance did not hide it properly, unless they hid it for someone to find and to benefit from it. After this discovery, the man goes to sell all he has in order to buy the entire field, legalising his find.

In the second parable, the merchant is deliberately seeking valuable pearls. He wants many but finds this particular one that is worth a lot and it becomes the centre of his focus. He sells all that he has to purchase it.

The central truth that is being taught in both parables is the immense value of the kingdom of God. The kingdom of God, put simply, is God's way of doing things. It means living a life under His kingship and receiving all the benefits that a king provides for his subjects. This far outweighs any sacrifice or inconvenience we might encounter on earth. It also outweighs any possessions and wealth we might have here on earth. The kingdom is so valuable to those who find it, whether by stumbling on it or as a result of a diligent search, that they are prepared to trade their lives for it. Jesus said, *"Whoever wants to be my disciple must deny themselves"* (**Matthew 16:24**). Self-denial is about self-sacrifice, and both men sacrificed their life savings for the pearl and the treasure. Jesus goes on to say, *"But whoever loses their life for me will find it"* (**Matthew 16:25**). Jesus assures us that we will not be at a loss if we sacrifice all we have for the kingdom.

This parable is important for instilling kingdom values and responsibilities. Both the men represent the attitude of a believer towards the kingdom. Believers should be ready to lose anything the world offers for the sake of the kingdom. It takes great faith to put all our confidence in the Word of God: it requires knowledge of the significance of the kingdom. Jesus also taught that we should seek first the kingdom of God (**Matthew 6:33**). This further indicates its value and significance for all who find it. Having found it, the men in the parables went and sold all they had in order to acquire it. The promise is, **"and all these things will be given to you as well"** (**Matthew 6:33**). We should treasure the kingdom of God and order our lives according to its principles.

REFLECTION TIME

Ask God to open your eyes to the treasure around you. Pray for the grace to let go of your own values and embrace the principles of the Kingdom of God.

19

THE LOST SHEEP

"*S*uppose *one of you has a hundred sheep and loses one of them. Doesn't he leave the ninety-nine in the open country and go after the lost sheep until he finds it? And when he finds it, he joyfully puts it on his shoulders and goes home. Then he calls his friends and neighbours together and says, 'Rejoice with me; I have found my lost sheep.' I tell you that in the same way there will be more rejoicing in heaven over one sinner who repents than over ninety-nine righteous persons who do not need to repent."* (**Luke 15:4–7**).

Jesus told this parable after He was accused of receiving sinners and eating with them. The scribes and Pharisees felt that they deserved the exclusive right to be around Jesus. They thought they were sinless and spotless. When Jesus concentrated on the sinners and the lost, the scribes and Pharisees were riled and resorted to complaining.

Jesus was sent for the sake of the lost, so He was accomplishing His purpose. The parable is quite satirical in that Jesus refers to them as the ninety-nine who did not need to repent. This exposes their pride and folly because the book of Romans clearly states that all have sinned and fallen short of the glory of God (**Romans 3:23**). The book of Isaiah also says, *"We all, like sheep, have gone astray, each of us has turned to our own way"* (**Isaiah 53:6**).

Jesus further mocked his accusers by saying that when one sheep is lost, the shepherd goes out in search for it, leaving the ninety-nine in the open country. Why would he leave sheep in dangerous open country to look for a sheep that has been lost in the same countryside? The attitude of the scribes and Pharisees meant that Jesus left them lost in their wilderness of pride and arrogance. They viewed others as sinners who did not deserve the love and embrace of a Saviour even though he had come for the lost.

We must not forget to look out for the lost, because we were also once lost. Jesus came for us all. If we are self-righteous, our attitude can leave us out of the Lord's plan. Jesus was happy to be among the lost, because He could shine the light of hope in their hearts through His love.

Many churches and believers today have disconnected themselves from the lost because they consider themselves to be clean. In the process they are left outside of God's grace. We must celebrate when lost people find forgiveness and mercy. Heaven rejoices when the lost sheep comes home. Those who repent are those who can be carried on the shoulders of the Saviour. *"Humble yourselves before the Lord, and he will lift you up"* (**James 4:10**).

The scribes and the Pharisees did not humble themselves, and they were left in the open country. *"God opposes the proud, but shows favour to the humble"* (James 4:6). We must be careful how we respond to God's work in the lives of others. He loves his sheep and He will go to great lengths to find them. If we love the Father, we will help Him find all the lost sheep of His household. Jesus' question to Peter was, *"Do you love me more than these?"* That love would be evidenced by the treatment of the sheep: *"Take care of my sheep"* (**John 21:15**).

REFLECTION TIME

Have you ever looked at others and considered yourself to be holier than they are? Have you ever looked at others and thought they were sinners but left them like that? God wants you to be compassionate and use your shoulders to bring them to the fold. Ask God to forgive you for your pride and for the occasions when you have been judgemental towards others. Pray for a humble heart and an understanding of heaven's attitude towards the lost.

20

THE UNMERCIFUL SERVANT

"Therefore the kingdom of heaven is like a certain king who wanted to settle accounts with his servants. And when he had begun to settle accounts, one was brought to him who owed him ten thousand talents. But as he was not able to pay, his master commanded that he be sold, with his wife and children and all that he had, and that payment be made. The servant therefore fell down before him, saying, 'Master, have patience with me, and I will pay you all.' Then the master of that servant was moved with compassion, released him, and forgave him the debt. "But that servant went out and found one of his fellow servants who owed him a hundred denarii; and he laid hands on him and took him by the throat, saying, 'Pay me what you owe!' So his fellow servant fell down at his feet and begged him, saying, 'Have patience with me, and I will pay you all.' And he would not, but went and threw him into prison till he should pay the debt." (**Matthew 18:23–30, NKJV**).

The unmerciful servant was forgiven an enormous debt, yet he failed to pass down the same mercy that he had received. To put it in perspective, this fellow owed ten thousand talents which is an enormous amount of money. His fellow servant only owed him a hundred denarii. A denarii was one day's wage for a labourer, so in essence, the fellow servant owed one hundred days' worth. The unmerciful servant, on the other hand, was forgiven a debt of ten thousand talents, which equates to six thousand denarii. His debt was six hundred times more. He went down on his knees and begged for patience. He was not only given patience, but his entire debt was cancelled. Yet this man could not accept a plea from his friend, even after he used the same words he himself had used to ask for pardon. He went further by throwing his friend into prison. How unmerciful!

In this parable Jesus seeks to reiterate the principle that we should forgive others because He has forgiven us. **Matthew 6:12** says, *"Forgive us our debts, as we also have forgiven our debtors."* We must forgive because we also want to be forgiven. It is wrong not to forgive when one has just been forgiven. The unmerciful servant was selfish and greedy. He was an opportunist who wanted to make money at the expense of his brother.

As Christians, we have a duty to follow in the footsteps of Jesus, who forgave us and gave His life for us. We cannot claim to be Christians if we fail to forgive those who trespass against us. That is hypocrisy. Paul consolidates this parable: *"Be kind and compassionate to one another, forgiving each other, just as in Christ God forgave you."* (**Ephesians 4:32**). The unmerciful servant not only failed to imitate his master; he also refused to hear the plea of a desperate man for mercy. He humiliated him and threw him into jail.

We may say we have no prisons into which we throw people, but some of us use our hearts as prisons. If you have not forgiven, all those whom you have not forgiven are captives in the prison of your heart. You can learn from this and begin to open your prison doors for your brothers to be free. Whatever it is that they owe you; the Bible requires that you forgive, as Christ forgave you. Whatever it is your brother or sister has done is not greater than the ten thousand talents that the Lord has forgiven you. Anything your brother or sister owes you will always be a hundred denarii and no more. It is in your interest to forgive because you owe the Lord much more, and you can never afford to pay God for Calvary.

Reflection Time

Look into your life and search for those instances where you have been unmerciful to others and ask the Lord to help you to forgive. Reflect on the many times the Lord has forgiven you. Let that soften your heart towards those who need your forgiveness. Consider the law of sowing and reaping: if you sow mercy, you will receive mercy. If you choose to sow unforgiveness that is what you will reap.

21

NEW CLOTH ON AN OLD COAT

"No one sews a piece of unshrunk cloth on an old garment, for the patch will pull away from the garment, making the tear worse." (**Matthew 9:16**) This parable is also told in **Mark 2:21** and **Luke 5:36**.

John the Baptist had come to tell the Jews that someone was coming who was to be followed as The Messiah. This person who was to come was Jesus (the new cloth). When Jesus came, He challenged some of the traditions and customs of the Jewish people. This proved difficult for the religious leaders who had become accustomed to certain behaviour and religious orders (the old garment). They wanted to embrace Jesus and also maintain their old ways. Jesus was telling them that the two could not be mixed. One had to be exchanged for the other. The old had to make way for the new. The problem was that the new came with principles and ways that were not readily accepted by the "oldies".

Sometimes we, too, struggle to change and break away from our old customs, resulting in us trying to marry the old and the new. Jesus warns that this is very destructive: *"No one sews a piece of unshrunk cloth on an old garment, for the patch will pull away from the garment, making the tear worse."* Refusal to adhere to this can make things worse for us. Jesus eventually pulled away from the temple (**John 4**).

The old garment has had time to shrink. The new will shrink as well, but that could actually damage the old, which is already delicate. Paul puts it this way: *"Therefore, if anyone is in Christ, the new creation has come: the old has gone, the new is here!"*

(**2 Corinthians 5:17**). Don't go back to your old ways after accepting Christ. Stick with the new: there is good reason for it.

Nicodemus was told a similar thing by Jesus when he asked, *"How can someone be born when they are old?" Jesus answered him by saying, "Flesh gives birth to flesh, but the Spirit gives birth to spirit"* (**John 3:4, 6**). You cannot put the two together. One will suffer.

The apostle Paul explains the same concept in **Galatians 5:16–17**: *"So I say, live by the Spirit, and you will not gratify the desires of the flesh. For the flesh desires what is contrary to the Spirit."* The flesh is like the old garment and the Spirit is like the new patch. If you try to mix them, the other will tear away, causing more harm. Paul goes further to explain the works of the flesh in verse 19–21, which are totally contrary to the fruit of the Spirit in verses 22 and 23.

Our new life in Jesus can never be mixed with our old ways and traditions. It's a total turnaround where we look for an entirely new garment instead of getting a little piece of a new garment sewn onto the old garment. Patches don't work in Jesus' kingdom. Salvation requires a total turnaround and calls for us to trust Jesus in our newfound faith.

Another example of a tear or damage of garments is **Ephesians 4:30**: *"And do not grieve the Holy Spirit of God."* We grieve the Spirit of God by trying to patch our old garments with new clothing – in other words by allowing carnality, which is a form of an old garment, in our newfound life of the Spirit.

REFLECTION TIME

Pray for transformation in the way you live your life. Don't mix the life of the kingdom with the life of the world. You are now a new creature in Christ. Walk daily in the newness of life.

22

LAMP ON A LAMPSTAND

"You are the light of the world. A town built on a hill cannot be hidden. Neither do people light a lamp and put it under a bowl. Instead they put it on its stand, and it gives light to everyone in the house." (**Matthew 5:14–15**).

Many towns and cities in Judea were founded on the summits or sides of mountains, and travellers could see them from afar and then find hope and guidance. Jesus was telling His disciples here that they were like a city on a hill in this lost world. A town built in an important location can be easily used as a point of reference, particularly when directing strangers who may not know the area.

The life of a disciple should be far reaching and should impact many areas. This illustration suggests a disciple's broader influence. It can also remind us that we cannot just live carelessly as believers and not be seen by the world we are trying to influence. This being the case, we should live our lives righteously as humble people, holy and pure, allowing our good conduct to be seen as though we are a town that is built on a hill.

We are the light of the world and must show godly character to the communities in which we live in order for the people within them to be reconciled to God and to one another. We receive our light from Jesus. As believers, we don't have inherent light in us. Instead, we have the reflective light that comes from Jesus who resides in us. That is why He wants us to abide in Him.

He also says that without Him we are nothing. We have no light without Him. He said He is the light of the world (**John 8:12**). After receiving Jesus in our hearts, His light shines through us for us to then reflect it to the world. This is why Jesus tells us that we are the light of the world. He has set us alight. He has switched the light on.

We must not hide under a table with this light because the world needs it. In Jesus' life, people saw the light, according to **Matthew 4:15–16**. *"Land of Zebulun and land of Naphtali, the Way of the Sea, beyond the Jordan, Galilee of the Gentiles – the people living in darkness have seen a great light; on those living in the land of the shadow of death a light has dawned."* Jesus went about doing good and preaching the kingdom. That is how the light dawned on people.

We are not saved just so that we can enjoy our lives; we are to be lights on the hills and mountains of our communities so that those who are in darkness can see the light and begin to walk towards it. You must look for a lampstand for your light to be seen. This lampstand could be your school; it could be your shop, your workplace, your neighbourhood or even your talent. Whatever it is, you should reflect the light of Jesus: *"Neither do people light a lamp and put it under a bowl."*

Now that we realise that the Lord has set us alight, we need to make sure that nothing comes between His light and us. There are many things that can switch off or obstruct that light. Jesus calls them "bowls". Examples of some of the bowls to avoid are found in **Philippians 2:14–15**. *"Do everything without grumbling or arguing, so that you may become blameless and pure, 'children of God without fault in a warped and crooked generation.' Then you will shine among them like stars in the sky."* So complaining can be a bowl, as can gossiping, hypocrisy, not forgiving, pride, doubt, insecurity, lies, sexual immorality, murmuring and all works of the flesh as listed in **Galatians 5:19–21**. These can obstruct and hinder the light from being seen.

REFLECTION TIME

Is your light shining? Are there any "bowls" in your life that are obstructing the light? How are you influencing others? Pray and ask the Lord to help you to be a light that shines brightly. Determine to be a godly example for others to follow.

23

THE GOOD SAMARITAN

This parable was told as an answer to a lawyer who wanted to know what he needed to do to inherit eternal life. He asked, *"And who is my neighbour?"* (**Luke 10:29**). This question was an attempt to limit the demands of the Law by suggesting that some people are our neighbours more than others. The learned lawyer wanted minimal and partial obedience. He wanted an obedience that was able to discriminate against those he disliked. Jesus, on the other hand, was looking for absolute obedience, where *"there is neither Jew nor Gentile"* (**Galatians 3:28**). Jesus reminded him that in order to make it into the kingdom we must love the Lord with our whole heart and love our neighbour as we love ourselves.

"A man was going down from Jerusalem to Jericho, when he was attacked by robbers. They stripped him of his clothes, beat him and went away, leaving him half-dead. A priest happened to be going down the same road, and when he saw the man, he passed by on the other side. So too, a Levite, when he came to the place and saw him, passed by on the other side. But a Samaritan, as he travelled, came where the man was; and when he saw him, he took pity on him. He went to him and bandaged his wounds, pouring on oil and wine. Then he put the man on his own donkey, brought him to an inn and took care of him. The next day he took out two denarii and gave them to the innkeeper. 'Look after him,' he said, 'and when I return, I will reimburse you for any extra expense you may have.'" (**Luke 10:30–35**)

After asking a question about who had done the right thing, Jesus told His listeners to go and do like the Samaritan. The words of the Samaritan depict Jesus Christ in that he said He would come again and reward the innkeeper for any expenses incurred in helping the injured man. **Revelation 22:12** reads, *"Look, I am coming soon! My reward is with me, and I will give to each person according to what they have done."* Jesus was talking about Himself and His heart towards strangers and the needy. Paul understood this in **1 Corinthians 11:1**: *"Follow my example, as I follow the example of Christ."* The Good Samaritan is a type of Christ that must be emulated!

There is another beauty in this story that Jesus wants us to see when working with people and God, who *"does not show favouritism"* (**Acts 10:34**). This parable is a typical reversal of stereotypes. The priest and the Levite were Jews who were supposed to live by the laws of God. They considered themselves to be good neighbours. They were, traditionally, the good fellows, while the Samaritan would have been a stranger, the one who compromised in religious matters – the bad guy, so to speak.

The Samaritan woman at the well in **John 4** had the same mind-set that thought that Jews could not be her neighbours. She was not even ready to give a needy Jew some water to drink. As badly as he may have been viewed, this Samaritan was, however, compassionate to the needs of others. He knew how to treat a neighbour in need. He had the heart of Jesus! The neighbour here was not his fellow man – or anyone he knew, it was a total stranger in need. As far as Jesus is concerned, all human beings are our neighbours, and they deserve our help when they are in need.

The parable sought to open the mind of a lawyer who thought he could only help and love a neighbour that he chose and tolerated. We do this often, and Jesus wants us to change and embrace all people.

REFLECTION TIME

How many people in need or trouble have you passed because you did not know them? How many have you not helped because you didn't know them? God wants us to love like He loves. Pray and ask God to forgive you where you turned a blind eye when you could have helped. Ask the Lord to help you to have a compassionate heart like the Good Samaritan as you journey in life.

24

THE EXPECTANT SERVANT

After the parable of the Rich Fool, Jesus used another parable to highlight the importance of preparing for His return. He used the analogy of a servant who stood in the middle of the night, waiting for his master to return from a wedding. To bring about the idea of expectancy, Jesus stated the need to open the door immediately when the master knocks. The immediate response showed that the servant had been ready and waiting.

"Be dressed ready for service and keep your lamps burning, like servants waiting for their master to return from a wedding banquet, so that when he comes and knocks they can immediately open the door for him" (**Luke12:35–36**). The idea of readiness is expressed in this last statement. It is very difficult to remain awake all night without knowing precisely what time the master will come. Nights were made for sleeping. *"So then, let us not be like others, who are asleep, but let us be awake and sober. Let us be expectant. For those who sleep, sleep at night, and those who get drunk, get drunk at night"* (**1 Thessalonians 5:6–7**).

As believers in Jesus, we must consistently expect His coming. This parable reminds us to stay ready. We must not drop our guard on our watch by falling asleep or getting drunk or falling into sinful behaviour. The Lord must find us ready and spotless. The Master will come at an hour we don't expect.

We must not be taken by surprise, because we have been warned. The question is, how seriously do we take such a warning? The early church took it seriously, from the account in Thessalonians. Though the day of the Lord will overtake the unsaved world and the unexpectant servants, it must not overtake you and me. It must not overtake believers. We should be expecting it and looking forward to it.

The fact that Christ could come at any moment should motivate unbelievers to accept His forgiveness, and believers to be expectant daily through their conduct and lifestyles. Because believers are well informed about these future events, they should not be spiritually asleep; rather they should watch and remain sober all the time. While many believers are hoping to go to heaven by virtue of salvation, many of them are not prepared to live every moment of their life as they are taught in the Scriptures. This shows that they are not ready. They are not vigilant and expectant of the Master's return. Readiness would imply soberness and a disciplined life that is alert to spiritual realities. We should be putting on the breastplate of faith and the basic aspects of the Christian life, such as obedience, holiness, faith, hope, love, forgiveness, sincerity and humility, daily. That is a prepared life. We should place our faith in God and give our love to God and others as we embrace the hope of salvation and live in the light of the Lord's return.

Many of us are taking this very lightly, but we should reconsider and begin to prepare our hearts for the Lord's return. Let us not be found sleeping. *"It will be good for those servants whose master finds them watching when he comes ... even if he comes in the middle of the night or towards daybreak"* (**Luke 12:37**).

REFLECTION TIME

How prepared are you for the coming of the Lord? Are you conscious of His return daily? What steps are you taking to make sure you are not found spiritually asleep? Ask the Holy Spirit to help you to stay alert and vigilant. Continue exercising spiritual disciplines daily.

25

THE GROWING SEED

Jesus said, *"This is what the kingdom of God is like. A man scatters seed on the ground. Night and day, whether he sleeps or gets up, the seed sprouts and grows, though he does not know how. All by itself the soil produces corn – first the stalk, then the ear, then the full grain in the ear. As soon as the corn is ripe, he puts the sickle to it, because the harvest has come"* (**Mark 4:26–29**).

This parable appears only in Mark's Gospel. Here Jesus likens the kingdom of God to a seed that is sown, grows in different stages, and eventually yields a harvest.

Plants grow and develop in a complex and very intricate process that humans do not fully understand. All man does is to plant the seed. The parable states that the man scatters the seed. He then sleeps and at night goes about his business during the day while the seed is growing under the ground. Eventually, the plant begins to show above ground, develops and is eventually harvested for the man to eat.

The seed is given power to grow by God. **Genesis 1:11–12** says, *"Then God said, 'let the land produce vegetation: seed-bearing plants and trees on the land that bear fruit with seed in it, according to their various kinds.' And it was so. The land produced vegetation: plants bearing seed according to their kinds and trees bearing fruit with seed in it according to their kinds."* Jesus is saying that the kingdom is as effective as the blessing of fruitfulness that was proclaimed in Genesis. Just as there is a harvest after sowing seed, there will be a harvest in the kingdom of God for those who sow the seeds of faith and obedience.

Jesus further points out that man does not even know how the seed develops and bears fruit, yet, when the harvest comes, he will gladly put the sickle to it and partake of the harvest. The kingdom is like that. We must continue to sow because the harvest is coming! Sometimes it may appear as though nothing is happening, but the seed is growing, and the promises of God will be fulfilled.

This is a parable of hope for those who have gone to bed without seeing signs of the harvest. It is also a parable of hope for those going about their day-to-day duties. The harvest is coming, and you will put your sickle to it and enjoy it. David, in Psalm 126, said, *"Those who go out weeping, carrying seed to sow, will return with songs of joy, carrying sheaves with them"* (verse 6). You will sing for joy when the harvest comes. Sometimes you will weep as you go out to sow that prayer; you will be weeping to sow that hospital visit; you may weep as you give the tithe, offering, and as you serve the Lord. The harvest will surely come. **Numbers 23:19** assures us of God's faithfulness: *"God is not human, that he should lie, not a human being, that he should change his mind. Does he speak and then not act? Does he promise and not fulfill?"*

Jesus said the kingdom of God is like a man who scatters seed in his field and sleeps. There are things we must learn to sleep over because we will never understand them. Certain things are too complex for us, but the Lord will enable the plant to grow. We will begin to see the ear and the corn from those complicated situations. Eventually, the harvest will come, and no one will tell you to put the sickle to it because you will know by yourself. As long as God has spoken, it will come to pass.

Plants continue to grow and to bear fruit and seeds, just the same as when God spoke in Genesis. Likewise, God's kingdom is growing, although we do not understand all that is happening. God is building His church; He is working out His promises for you. He promised to bless you, so you are blessed and you will continue to be blessed. You may not know how, but one day your harvest will be ready, and you will rejoice.

REFLECTION TIME

Are you losing heart? Are you getting tired of doing good? Are you wondering when your harvest will come? Do not give up. Ask God to strengthen you and to help you focus on His word and promises. Continue to sow. The kingdom is like seeds that are scattered. Scatter on and see what the Lord will do. Galatians 6:9 instructs us not to become weary in doing good for we shall reap in due course if we do not grow weary. Guard your heart against growing weary!

26

THE TALENTS

"
A t that time the kingdom of heaven would be like this. Once there was a man who was about to leave home on a trip; he called his servants and put them in charge of his property. He gave to each one according to his ability: to one he gave five thousand gold coins, to another he gave two thousand, and to another he gave one thousand. Then he left on his trip. The servant who had received five thousand coins went at once and invested his money and earned another five thousand. In the same way the servant who had received two thousand coins earned another two thousand. But the servant who had received one thousand coins went off, dug a hole in the ground, and hid his master's money." (**Matthew 25:14–18, GNT**)

If you read the entire passage you will realise that the last servant was driven by fear. He thought the master was testing him, so he thought, "I will hide this treasure and give it back to him as it is, as I don't want trouble." The man was not innovative. He did not see potential. He was not creative. He could not take advantage of the capital he had been offered. He lost out on an opportunity to transform his life. Sometimes opportunities do not come back. We must be shrewd and act in faith. The Bible says, *"The fear of man brings a snare, but whoever trusts in the Lord shall be safe."* (**Proverbs 29:25**). The man was afraid, so he hid his treasure in the ground. In addition, he risked losing that money because someone could have found the treasure.

Everything in life is risky, and we must learn to take risks in faith. The master did not tell these men what to do with the gold coins. He merely gave them and went away. The first and second servant immediately saw an opportunity and grabbed it. This worked and they doubled their capital, while the other did nothing.

The master had given to them according to their abilities. This means the last servant had the ability to double the thousand coins he was given. We all have the ability to double the gifts God has given us, but some of us are reluctant to take the step because we are afraid.

The lesson to learn from this parable is that we must use what God has given us or we might lose it. This includes abilities and spiritual gifts as well as material possessions. We must learn to use them all for the glory of God. **Luke 9:24** says, *"For if you want to save your own life, you will lose it, but if you lose your life for my sake, you will save it."* The last servant wanted to save his integrity and the investment he was given. Unfortunately, he lost it. We must learn to walk in faith, have confidence in our abilities and do our best to multiply and increase them.

The master wants us to be creative, innovative and fruitful. Businessmen want productive people. God wants productive people. The master did not see his servant as a coward; he saw laziness. He saw him as wicked and lazy: *"But his lord answered and said to him, 'you wicked and slothful servant! You knew that I reap where I have not sown and gather where I scattered no seed? Then you ought to have invested my money with the bankers"* (**Matthew 25:26–27**). Sometimes we hide our laziness and wickedness behind fear.

God wants us to grow what He has put in us. Those who do so will be honoured. We must make an effort to utilise our gifts, because when Jesus comes back He will want to know what we have done with the gifts He has given us. **Romans 12:3** reminds us that *"God has dealt to each one a measure of faith"* (NKJV). God has given all of us a certain amount of faith, according to our abilities, and He will be looking at what we did with them.

Jesus has already warned that He will be looking for this on His return: *"But will the son of man find faith on earth when he returns?"*(**Luke 18:8**) Why would Jesus want to find faith when He has not given it to us? We must use our faith and abilities to glorify God and to be a blessing to others.

REFLECTION TIME

Are you using your gifts to bless others? Do you serve in any way in your church? Are you doubling or growing the gifts that God has given you? Can He trust you with more? Pray that God will help you to be a faithful steward of the gifts and talents He has given you. Pray that you may be fruitful in all you do.

27

THE TWO DEBTORS

"And Jesus answering said to him, 'Simon, I have something to say to you.' And he answered, 'Say it, Teacher.'" (**Luke 7:40**) Jesus went on to say something in connection with the thoughts of Simon that were a result of him watching a prostitute kissing the feet of Jesus in verses 38 and 39. This parable was, in fact, a response to a man who thought he was more righteous than the prostitute.

Simon thought Jesus did not know what He was doing. "*If this man were a prophet, he would have known who and what sort of woman this is who is touching him, for she is a sinner*" (**Luke 7:39**). This was very dangerous and arrogant: Simon was even questioning the credentials of Jesus' prophetic ministry because He allowed a grateful woman to touch him.

In His response, Jesus said, "*Simon, I have something to say to you.*" The confident Pharisee urged Jesus on: "*Say it, Teacher.*" Jesus continued, "*a certain moneylender had two debtors. One owed five hundred denarii, and the other fifty. When they could not pay, he cancelled the debt of both. Now which of them will love him more?' Simon answered, 'The one, I suppose, for whom he cancelled the larger debt.*'"

Jesus then equated the one who owed 500 denarii to the woman who was appreciating Jesus and showering Him with her tears, and the one who owed 50 denarii to Simon, his host (verses 44–48). Simon could not see the potential of Jesus to restore the woman's life by His grace. He labelled her, forgetting that he was a sinner as well. There is a danger of believers becoming too familiar with God's grace and failing to appreciate and worship God for what He has done for us, because we label ourselves as better and more deserving than others.

Jesus knew well the reputation of the woman, but He was more interested in what the woman could become through the grace of God. This is how we must view people we minister to. This is how we should view our brothers who are weak. What can the grace of God do to change their lives? We must not compare them with ourselves, because we have also been forgiven, just as they have been. If we understand forgiveness, we should not go beyond that to begin to compare how much we have been forgiven. In His grace, God has chosen to forgive. We must not fall into the trap of thinking God does not know what He is doing. He does, and He wants to tell us something about His reasons for allowing certain things.

"I have something to say to you." "Your sins are forgiven." It does not matter who knows that you are a sinner (verse 39). The grace of God has come to forgive all those who are prepared to embrace His love, no matter their state. *"You did not anoint my head with oil, but she has anointed my feet with ointment. Therefore I tell you, her sins, which are many, are forgiven – for she loved much"* (**Luke 7:46–47**). The lesson is in these words, and in Jesus' response to the thoughts of the Pharisee.

We must not judge other people's love and service for God. The woman knew her life and she knew what had happened in her heart. Jesus' point is that the amount of love showered on the Saviour is normally in direct proportion with one's sense of the gravity of the sins that the Master has forgiven. The woman knew she had been forgiven much, and she did not care what the Pharisee thought about her, and Jesus supported her.

REFLECTION TIME

Forgiveness comes from the Master. He forgives as He wills. Pray that you may learn to accept God's grace towards others. Pray for humility. Do not question God in His dealings with people. Ask God for the grace to be grateful for your own forgiveness, no matter how small, because you could still never pay for it.

28

THE RICH FOOL

Jesus told this parable after a young man asked Him to tell his brother to share an inheritance with him. Jesus was aware of the complications and possible fallout between these brothers and He chose not to be involved directly. He nonetheless offered this parable, with the hope that the brothers would see sense and treat each other well.

"The ground of a certain rich man yielded an abundant harvest. He thought to himself, 'What shall I do? I have no place to store my crops.' Then he said, 'This is what I'll do. I will tear down my barns and build bigger ones, and there I will store my surplus grain. And I'll say to myself, "You have plenty of grain laid up for many years. Take life easy; eat, drink and be merry."' But God said to him, 'You fool! This very night your life will be demanded from you. Then who will get what you have prepared for yourself?' This is how it will be with whoever stores up things for themselves but is not rich towards God." (**Luke 12:16–21**)

This parable raises a number of questions. Jesus did not mean people should not make financial investments. The issue Jesus was highlighting was the selfishness that we exhibit sometimes. The rich fool was focused on himself: "I will build bigger barns; I will relax; I will eat; I will drink; I will be merry!" This is the attitude of many of us today concerning our possessions. Rather than putting them in storage for years at exorbitant costs, Jesus is suggesting that we share with those who do not have as much. It is not wise to prepare for *"many years"* when we could assist family and friends who are suffering now. We are not certain about being alive for those future years for which we hoard.

This man was consumed by himself: his world revolved around himself. This can be seen by the six 'I's in this short account. Jesus called him a fool because of his selfishness. Selfishness makes us concentrate on ourselves; generosity makes us consider others. When we use our resources to bless others, we begin to be wise in the eyes of God, and that is what it means to be rich towards God. When our souls are removed from this material world, we transition to another world that is rich towards God. We prepare for that world by using our resources to bless others in this world.

The brothers who were fighting over the inheritance were being shown this other side of life. While Jesus did not interfere with their dispute, He showed them that the world could end at any time and they could find themselves poor in the life to come.

May we learn to spend our resources building things of eternal value. We could leave this world at any time, therefore it is important to be clear on what to do with our earthly possessions, and not just stack them up for a future we might not see.

God's judgement on the rich fool was clear. We should prepare for the next life using our earthly possessions. We cannot take them with us to eternity. What we own in this world will be of no value to us after this earth.

The rich young man became poor at the point of his death. All earthly wealth is temporary. Jesus warned about this in **Matthew 6:19–20**: *"Do not lay up for yourselves treasures on earth ... but lay up for yourselves treasures in heaven."* Paul says the same to Timothy: *"For we brought nothing into the world, and we can take nothing out of it"* (**1 Timothy 6:7**; see also verses 6–10). Paul continues to warn the rich fools of this world in verses 17–19: *"Command those who are rich in this present world not to be arrogant nor to put their hope in wealth, which is so uncertain, but to put their hope in God, who richly provides us with everything for our enjoyment. Command them to do good,* *to be rich in good deeds, and to be generous and willing to share. In this way they will lay up treasure for themselves as a firm foundation for the coming age, so that they may take hold of the life that is truly life."*

We must learn to be wise with our earthly wealth so that we will not stand before God empty handed. Another admonition is given in **James 5:1-6**. Do not boast about tomorrow in your wealth; the Lord may just call you tonight.

REFLECTION TIME

With what parts of this parable can you identify? What would you do if you had great wealth? What parts of this story make you uncomfortable? Does this parable in any way suggest that it's wrong to plan for retirement or to save money? Is your giving just about you and your immediate family? Ask the Lord to help you not to be selfish. Identify people you can help. Give away what you are not using. Invest in that which has eternal value.

29

THE WISE AND FOOLISH BUILDERS

I once read an article about a massive shopping mall that collapsed and killed people who were busy constructing it in Kwazulu Natal, South Africa. Investigations found that the owner had not followed correct procedures. He cut corners in order to save money and people died as the building collapsed due to inferior building material, poor workmanship, and poor foundations. Other than the death of innocent lives, valuable resources in bricks, cement, water, steel reinforcements, and valuable time were lost. The same happened in India. How you build, where you build, and the quality of materials you use to build matters.

That is why construction is a heavily regulated industry. Building a house requires wisdom and strict adherence to rules regulating the foundations in order to protect lives. Building a big structure on the wrong foundation is risky. Jesus alluded to this in his parables when he talked about the kingdom of God. He taught how some people will lose their "buildings" if they don't adhere to the standards of the kingdom to build their eternal house. *"Therefore whoever hears these sayings of mine and does them, I will liken him to a wise man who built his house on a rock: and the rain, descended, the floods came, and the winds blew and beat on that house; and it did not fall, for it was founded on a rock. But everyone who hears these words of mine, and does not do them, will be like a foolish man who built his house on sand; and the rain descended, the floods came, and the winds blew and beat on that house; and it fell. And great was its fall."* **Matthew 7:24-27**. This parable is repeated in **Luke 6:47-49**, the key point here is that the difference in the two houses was not their outward appearance but the foundation on which they were built.

Pharisees and Scribes appeared to be righteous like Jesus from the outside but they were different houses from how and where they were built. The foundations are what made the difference! The house on a rock symbolises a faith and a lifestyle that is founded on a proper relationship with Jesus Christ. *"And I also say to you that you are Peter, and on this rock I will build my church, and the gates of hell shall not prevail against it."* (**Matthew 16:18**). The rock is the relationship with Jesus. *"All drank the same spiritual drink. For they drank of that Spiritual Rock that followed them, and that Rock was Christ."* (**1 Corinthians 10:4**). This Rock is also mentioned in **1 Peter 2:4-8**. The house built on this rock is the house that will stand the test of Christ's judgement but the house built on sand will fail the test according to this parable and **1 Corinthians 3:12-15**. *"Now if anyone builds on this foundation with gold, silver, precious stones wood, hay, straw each one's work will become clear; for the day will declare it, because it will be revealed by fire and the fire will test each one's work, of what sort it is. If anyone's work which he has built on it endures, he will receive a reward. If any one's work is burned, he will suffer loss..."*

We build on a rock by following and living according to the teachings of Jesus. *"Therefore whoever hears these words of mine and does them. I will liken to a wise man who built his house on a rock."* (Verse 24). The mall in South Africa collapsed, the other building in India collapsed as well. But there are more serious house "collapses" that will come if we continue to despise the instructions of Jesus. Great will be the fall. We must learn to fully heed the warnings Jesus gave us through His parables. It will not be long before certain buildings crumble but we have been warned on how we can be wise builders. Which type of a builder are you? Wise or foolish? Short cuts are not going to help you. God will test everything.

REFLECTION TIME

How are you living your life? You may not realise it but you are building a house that shall be tested one day. Ask God for the grace to be wise in how you build. Wise builders hear the sermons and teachings of Jesus and do them. Pray that you may be a doer of the word as James teaches. (**James 1:22**).

30

WEEDS AMONG GOOD PLANTS

"The kingdom of heaven is like a man who sowed good seed in his field. But while everyone was sleeping, his enemy came and sowed weeds among the wheat, and went away. When the wheat sprouted and formed ears, then the weeds also appeared. The owner's servants came to him and said, 'Sir, didn't you sow good seed in your field? Where then did the weeds come from?' 'An enemy did this,' he replied. The servants asked him, 'Do you want us to go and pull them up?' 'No,' he answered, 'because while you are pulling up the weeds, you may uproot the wheat with them. Let both grow together until the harvest.'" (**Matthew 13:24–30**)

There are a number of lessons to learn from this passage. First is the fact that weeds closely resemble wheat, but are poisonous to human beings. They are not good plants and they are the planting of Satan. They are indistinguishable from wheat until the final fruit appears on the wheat. They are not always easy to identify. Weeds do not bear fruit! Farmers would strip out weeds just before harvesting the wheat. Weeds could be equivalent to false brethren, as seen in **Galatians 2:4**: *"This matter arose because some false believers had infiltrated our ranks."* Weeds were secretly planted in the night while the farmer was sleeping.

The church will always have weeds if we do not prayerfully and diligently conduct our fellowship. There will be a harvest that will distinguish between the weeds and the wheat. This harvest is the judgement, and it shows us that the enemy will never win. Jesus said, *"I will build my church, and the gates of Hades will not overcome it"* (**Matthew 16:18**).

The reapers of the harvest will know the difference between weeds and wheat. There will be no confusion, and no weed will make it into the kingdom. Weeds can make noise and try to accuse the brethren (**Galatians 2:4**) but it will not work for long. The Bible teaches us that God knows the hearts of men: *"The Lord looks at the heart"* (**1 Samuel 16:7**). He can tell truth from hypocrisy and separate them easily. *"Nothing in all creation is hidden from God's sight. Everything is uncovered and laid bare before the eyes of him to whom we must give account"* (**Hebrews 4:13**).

The other point to note is that sometimes we do the right thing but the devil comes in to spoil. If we fail to see the hand of the enemy when weeds begin to appear, we begin to fight and accuse one another. This will only perpetuate a situation where we try to pull up the weeds, but in the process we risk uprooting the wheat as well. We must allow God to take care of certain matters, understanding that at the end all truth will be revealed. We must learn to *"Let both grow together."* The challenge is that there is much discomfort when weeds and wheat grow together. Jesus has already warned us that the enemy will sow weeds at certain times in our lives.

Another thing to learn is the danger of sleeping when we should be watching. We can miss the Lord's coming by sleeping, and the Bible teaches that the enemy can attack us or spoil our crop if we sleep on duty. Sleeping on duty is a dismissible offence in the workplace. The Bible tells us that, *"he who watches over you will not slumber; indeed, he who watches over Israel will neither slumber nor sleep. The Lord watches over you … the sun will not harm you by day, nor the moon by night"* (**Psalm 121:3–7**). This is how seriously the Lord takes His watch over you. He does not sleep because He is aware that it is during sleep that the enemy sows weeds. We must learn diligence and watchfulness from God as seen in **Psalm 121**.

Diligence will help us avoid the pain of having to watch our wheat grow together with weeds. Imagine the waste of resources as weeds consume all the nutrients, just to be burned! What a waste! Diligence will help us avoid fellowship with hypocrites who want to see us destroyed. Weeds come when we are sleeping. They often appear when we least expect them, so we must be on our guard. We must guard jealously the faith and salvation God has given us. We must be alert to the fact that the enemy wants to sow division. When he does, he goes away, leaving us to face the consequences. We must be alert and watchful so that we do not open the door for the enemy.

REFLECTION TIME

What kind of seeds are you sowing? How seriously are you guarding your heart? How about your prayer life: are you sleeping? Your study of the Word: are you sleeping? Service and giving in the church: are you sleeping? Ask God to help you to wake up and begin to live by your faith and conviction. Pray that you do not become like weeds that will be uprooted.

ABOUT THE AUTHOR

Osien Sibanda is an ordained minister of the Gospel. He is the senior pastor of God's House International Centre Bristol. He is an inspiring, gifted teacher of the Word of God. His experience in working with different denominations and people from various cultural backgrounds has broadened his capacity to work effectively with people. Pastor Osien is a conference speaker and a mentor of men. His passion is to see men taking responsibility in their homes, communities and churches. Pastor Osien was involved in church planting in Southern Africa and has done pastoral work in the UK. He also served as the Chairperson of Agape Husbands for four successive years in Johannesburg, South Africa.

He graduated with a Masters degree in Practical Theology from the University of Wales-Bangor. He is the author of *The Principles and Practice of Giving*, *The God Told Me Syndrome*, *Count the Cost*, *The Value Of Kindness* and *The Pursuit Of God: 30 Day Devotional*. Pastor Osien is married to Fatima and they are blessed with two lovely daughters, Ayanda and Realeboga.

OTHER BOOKS BY SIBANDA PUBLISHING

 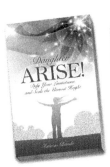  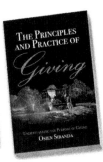

The Fragrance of a Godly Woman
by Fatima Sibanda
ISBN: 978-0-9561175-0-2

Daughter Arise! Defy Your Limitations and Scale the Utmost Height
by Fatima Sibanda
ISBN: 978-0-9561175-4-0

The Value of Kindness
by Osien Sibanda
ISBN: 978-0-9561175-6-4

The Principles and Practice of Giving
by Osien Sibanda
ISBN: 978-0-9561175-1-9

The God Told Me Syndrome
by Osien Sibanda
ISBN: 978-0-9561175-2-6

Count the Cost
by Osien Sibanda
ISBN: 978-0-9561175-3-3

Your Path is Becoming Brighter
by Fatima Sibanda
ISBN: 978-0-9561175-7-1

For more information please contact info@sibandapublishing.com

Lightning Source UK Ltd.
Milton Keynes UK
UKOW05f1037210217
294917UK00001B/124/P